GET A <u>FREE</u> COLORING BOOK

Dogs? Unicorns? Cars? Superheroes? Fashion?... The choice is yours!

Your feedback means an incredible amount to us. To say thanks for leaving us a review on Amazon we'd like to offer you a FREE COLORING BOOK from our collection!

How to get your book

Simply leave an honest review of this coloring book on Amazon, then visit captaincolouringbook.com/claim to claim your free downloadable coloring book.

First, scan this to leave a review

Then scan this to claim your reward

www.captaincolouringbook.com

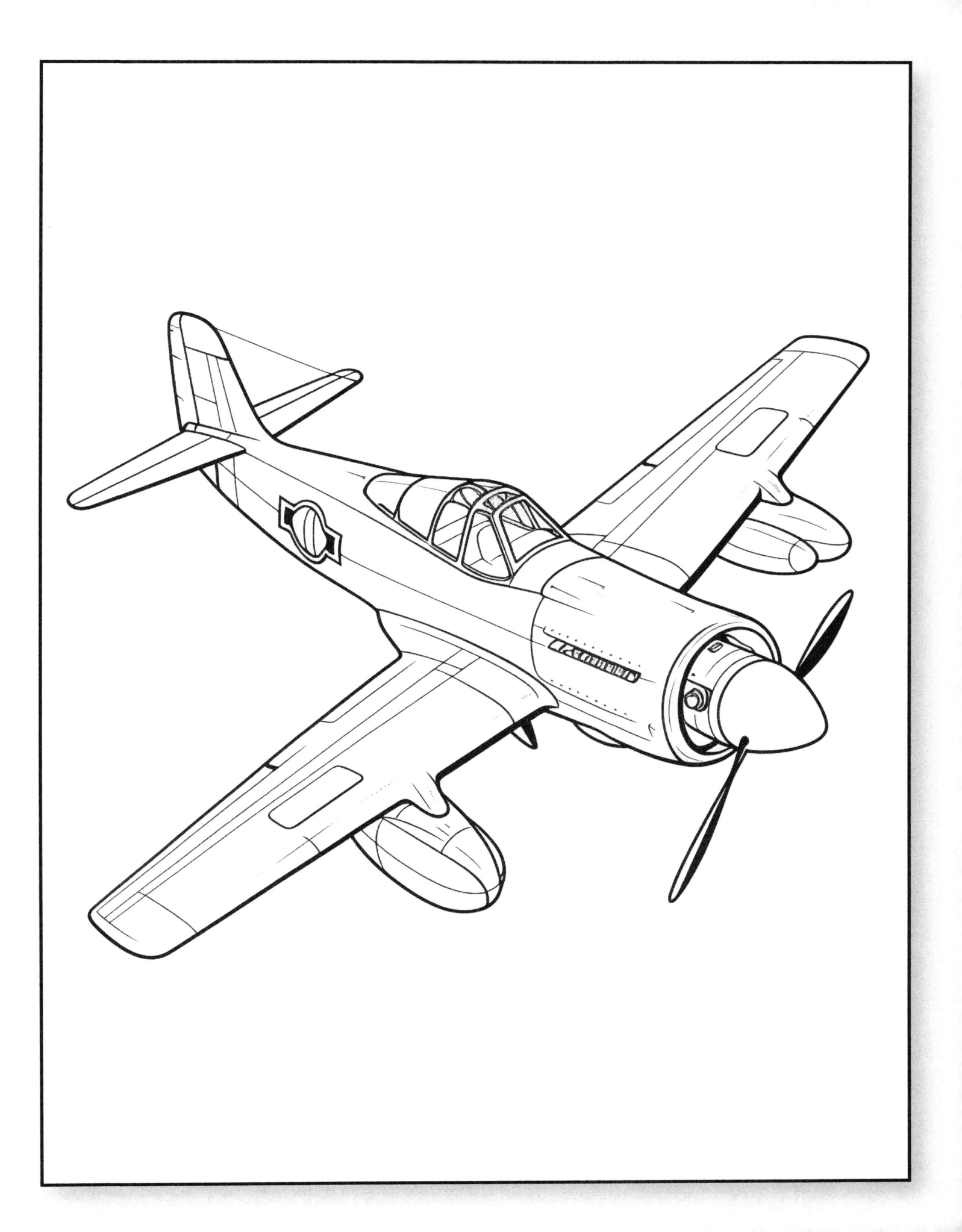

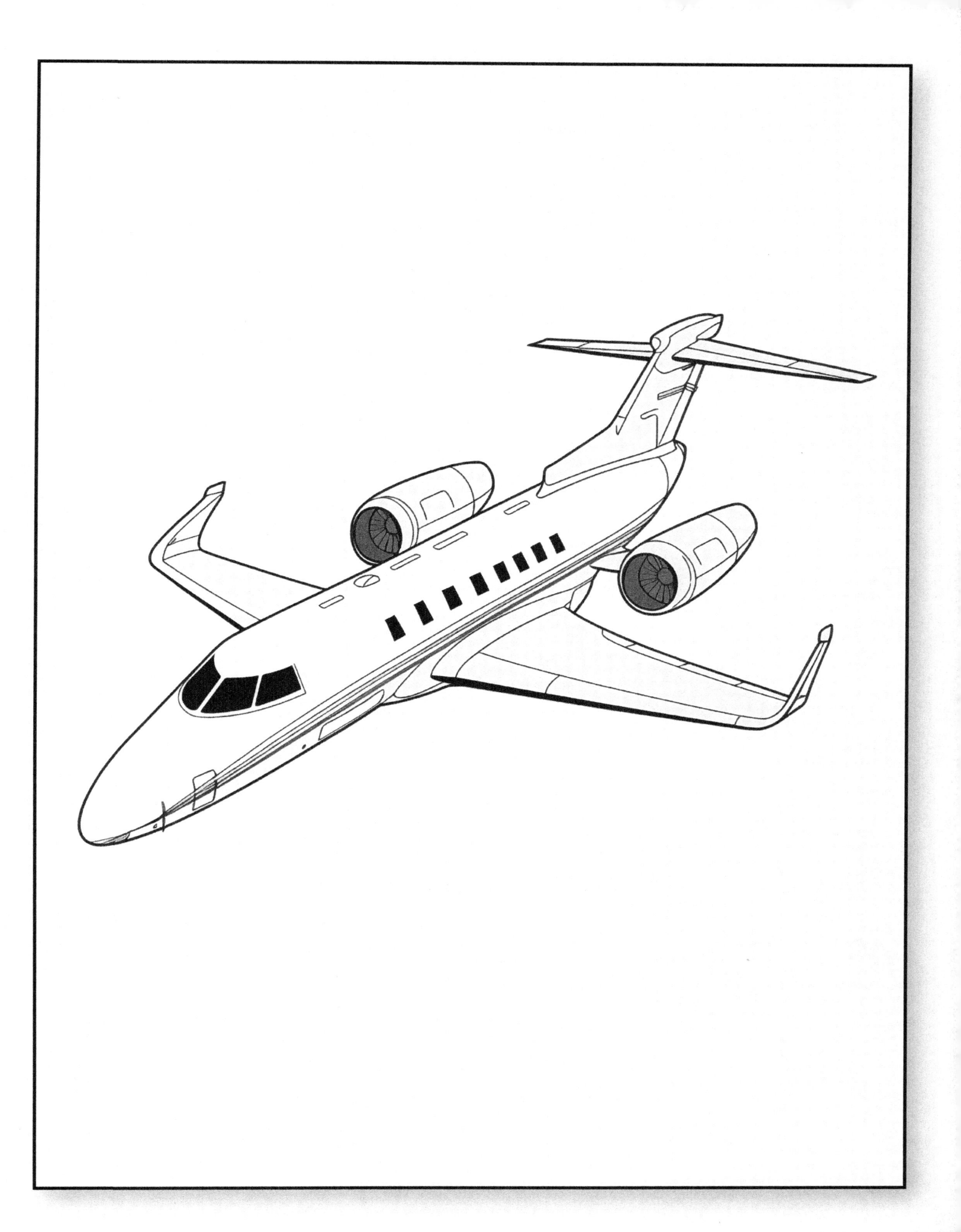

ALSO AVAILABLE FROM CAPTAIN COLOURING BOOK

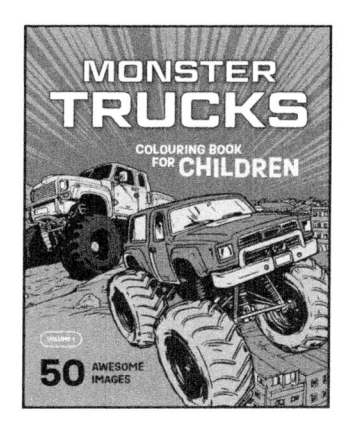   

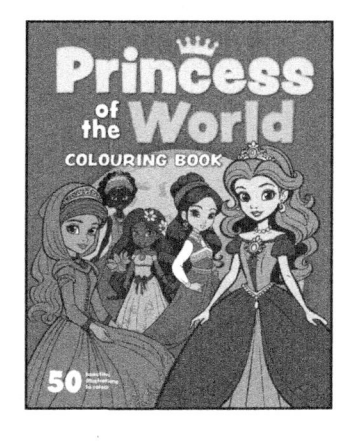   

Plus many more! To see the full collection visit
www.captaincolouringbook.com

Printed in Great Britain
by Amazon